Christmas
Impressions

Creative Carol Settings for Solo Piano

Victor Labenske

Editor: Lloyd Larson
Music Engraving: MacMusic, Inc.
Cover Design: Patti Jeffers

ISBN: 978-0-7877-4395-6

lillenas
PUBLISHING COMPANY

www.lorenz.com

Foreword

Thoughts of Christmas bring to mind joy, music (with rehearsals and performances), family, gifts, frantic shopping, and then finally, a slower pace. I am blessed with the privilege of being able to write Christmas music. This act of writing and reflecting on the wonderful words of these Christmas carols helps me refocus my attention on the Important One of Christmas: our Savior, Jesus Christ. The cultural trappings of Christmas melt away and Christ meets us, sharing His grace, healing, peace, love, and joy which we are called to share with our world.

I pray that this collection will be a tangible way for me to share Christ with you. And then my hope is that you will pass along this music to others as you play, sharing with them the gifts that Christ has given you.

— *Victor Labenske*

About the Arranger

Victor Labenske is professor of music at Point Loma Nazarene University in San Diego, California, where he teaches courses in piano and composition. A *summa cum laude* graduate of PLNU, he earned his Master's Degree in piano performance at the University of Missouri–Kansas City, Conservatory of Music where he studied with Joanne Baker. He also earned the Doctor of Musical Arts in piano performance at the University of Southern California where he studied with Stewart Gordon.

Victor has been honored with such distinctions as playing in the opening ceremonies of the 1984 Olympic Games and being named an Academic All-American Scholar. His compositional output of over 500 published compositions and arrangements includes sacred piano collections, educational piano music, and music for violin and piano, voice and piano, and handbells. Dr. Labenske remains active as a concert artist both as soloist and as a collaborative performer, and enjoys presenting sacred concerts with his wife, soprano, Judith Spaite Labenske. The Labenskes have two children, Karlin and Kristofer.

Contents

O Come, All Ye Faithful

Attr. to JOHN F. WADE
Arr. by Victor Labenske

Majestically ♩ = ca. 126

Pedal ad lib

mf legato

cresc.

f

dim.

rit.

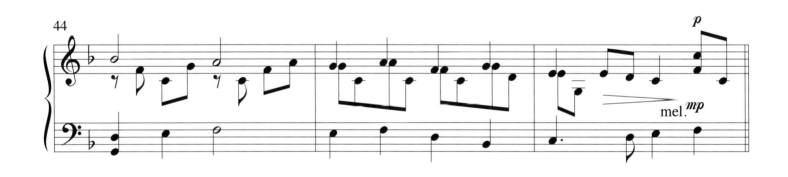

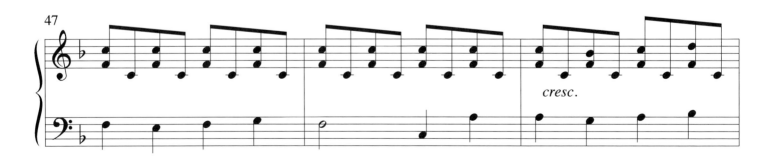

In the Bleak Midwinter

GUSTAV T. HOLST
Arr. by Victor Labenske

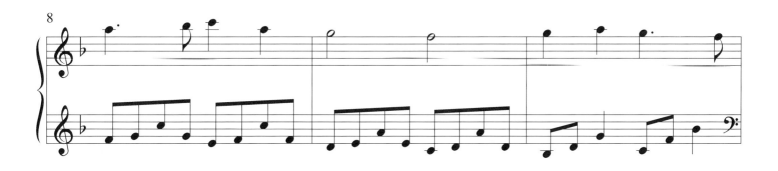

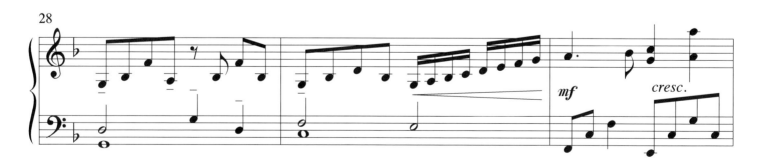

Good Christian Friends, Rejoice

Traditional German Melody
Arr. by Victor Labenske

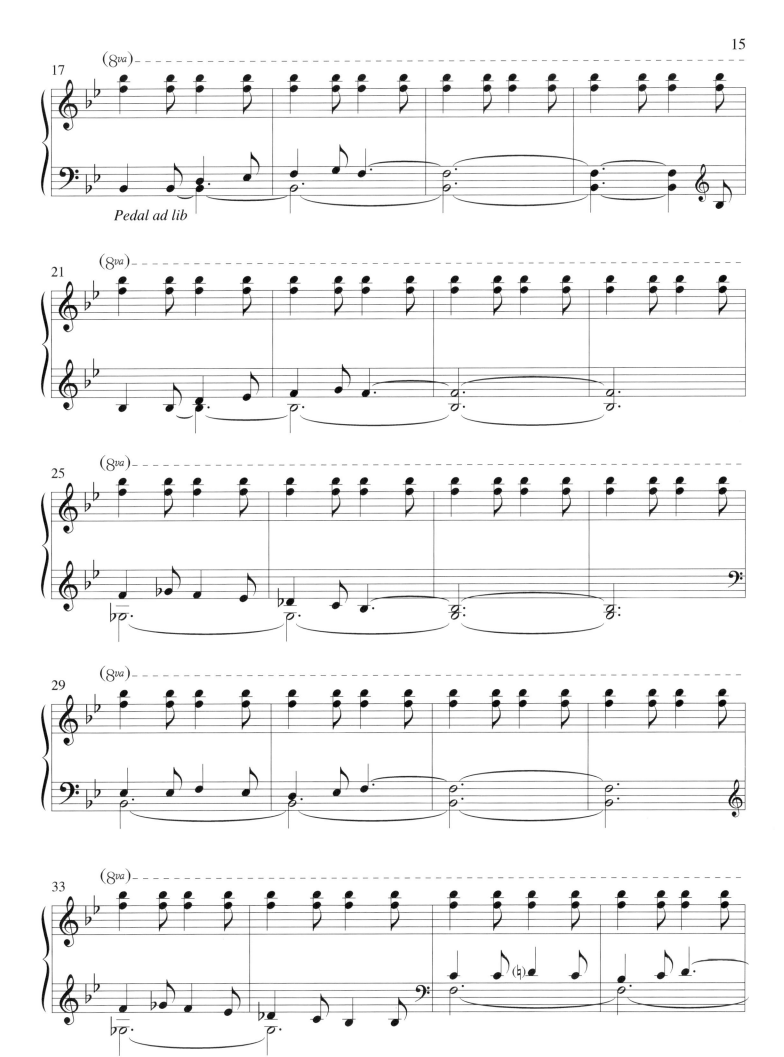

Pedal ad lib

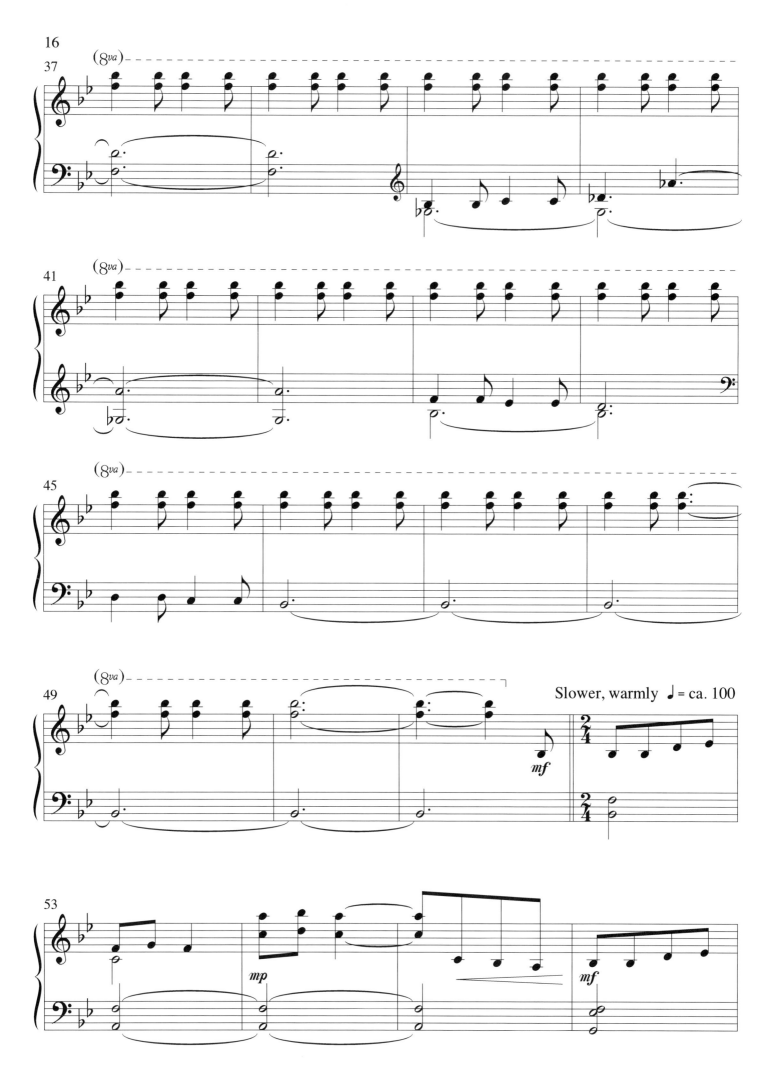

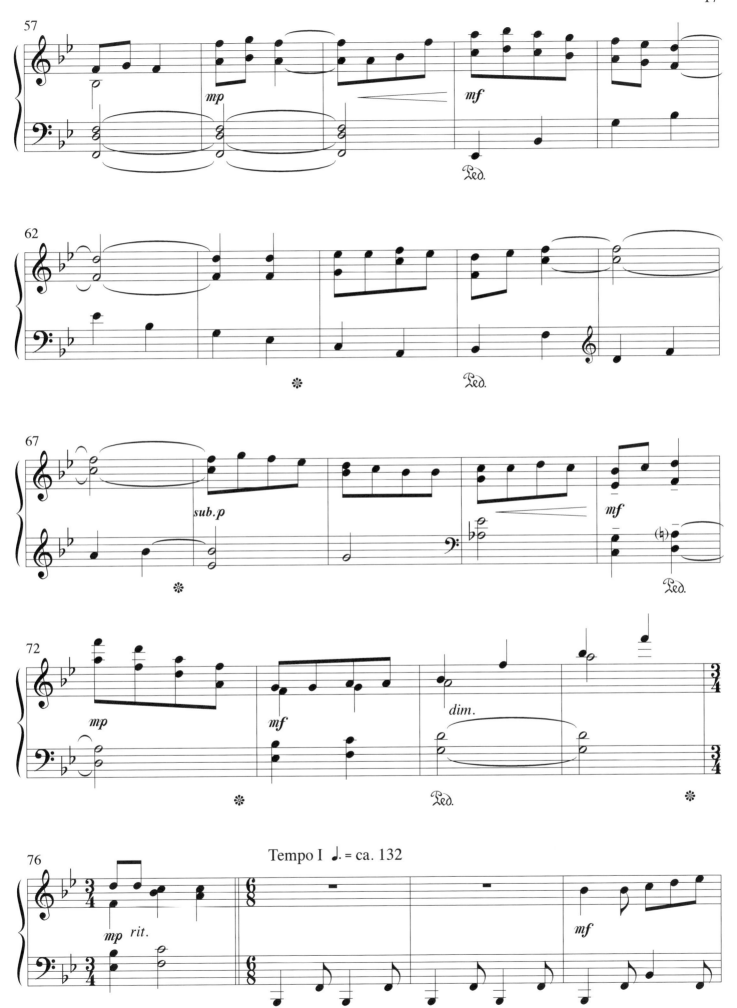

I Saw Three Ships

Traditional English Melody
Arr. by Victor Labenske

Brightly ♩. = ca. 120

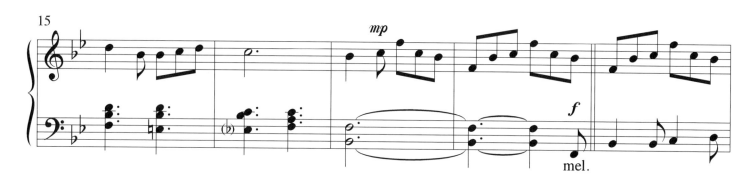

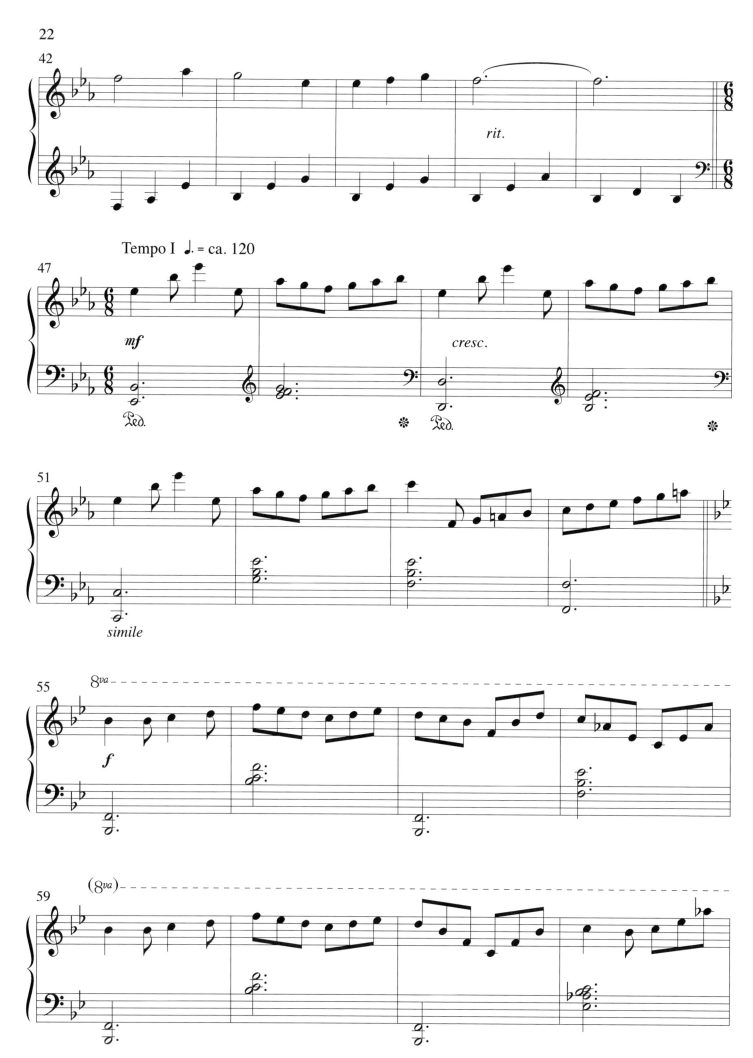

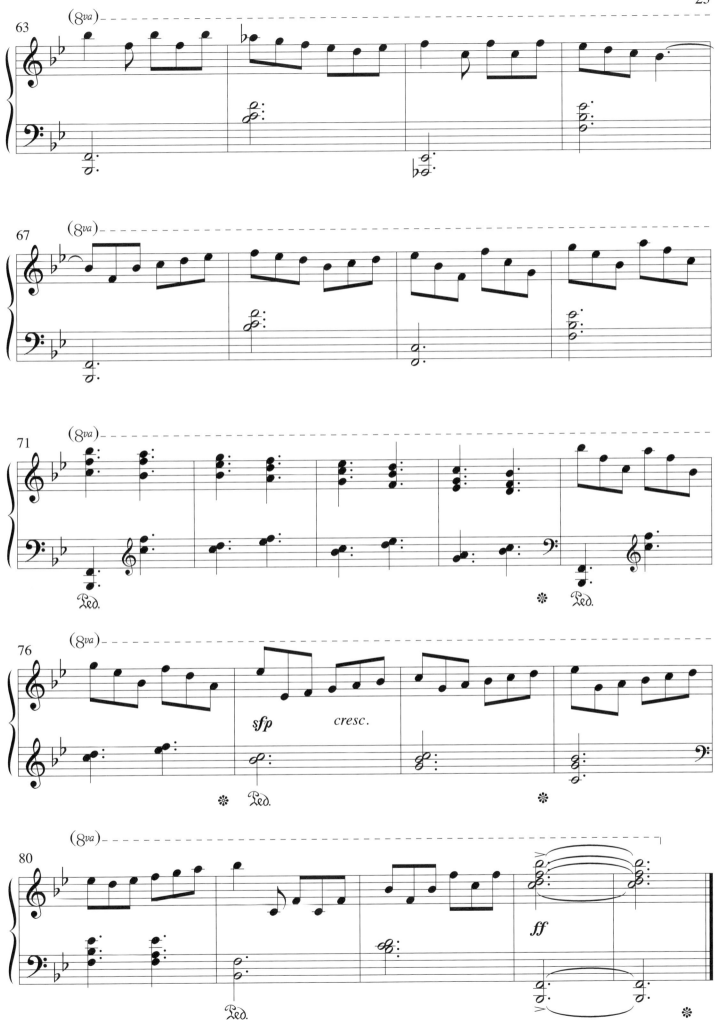

It Came upon the Midnight Clear

RICHARD S. WILLIS
Arr. by Victor Labenske

God Rest Ye Merry, Gentlemen

Traditional English Melody
Arr. by Victor Labenske

Do Not
Photocopy

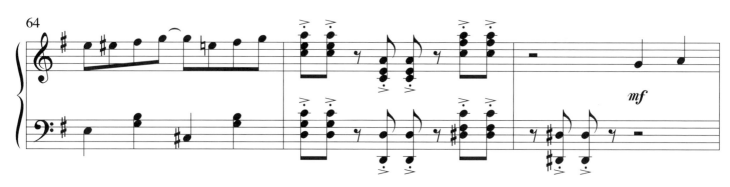

Angels We Have Heard on High

Traditional French Melody
Arr. by Victor Labenske

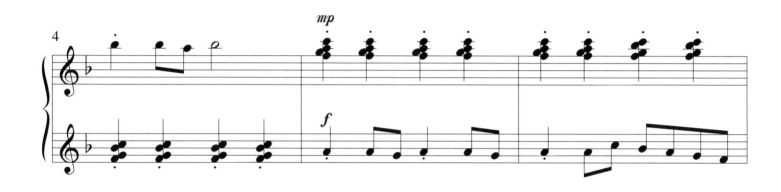

Do Not
Photocopy

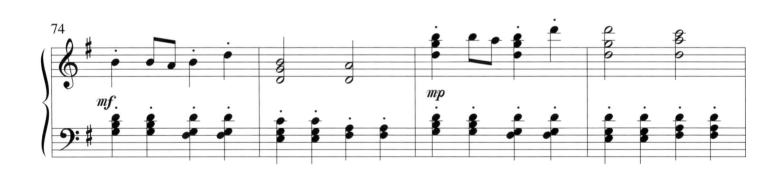

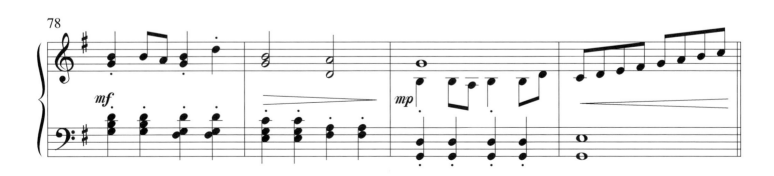

Ding Dong! Merrily on High

Traditional French Carol
Arr. by Victor Labenske

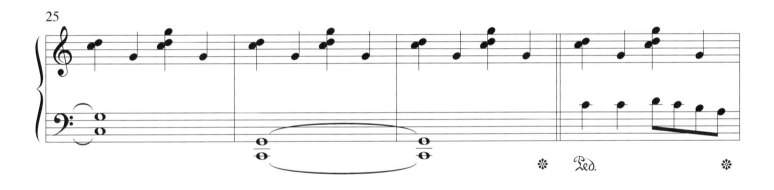

Come, Thou Long-expected Jesus

ROWLAND H. PRICHARD
Arr. by Victor Labenske

Yearning ♩. = ca. 60

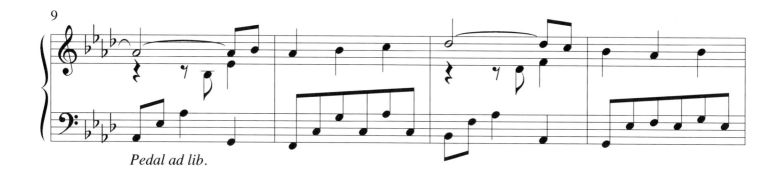

Do Not
Photocopy

The First Noel

W. Sandy's *Christmas Carols*, 1833
Arr. by Victor Labenske

With wonder ♩= ca. 116

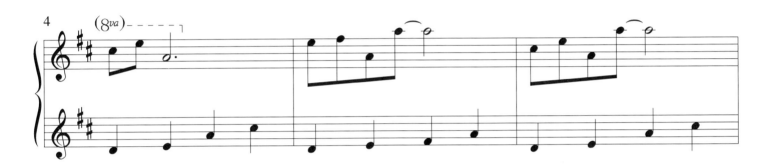

simile

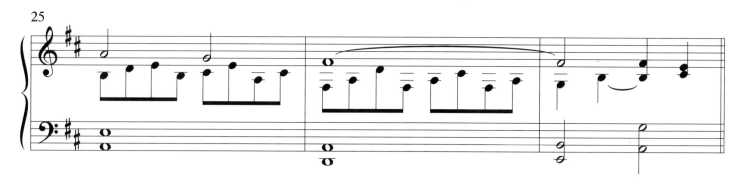

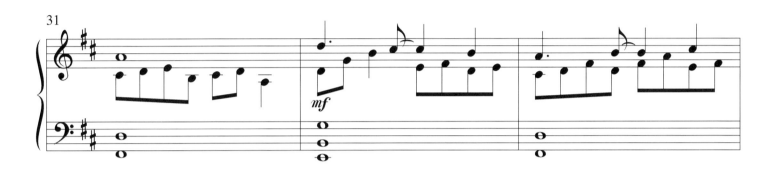